HORSE
DICTIONARY

An A to Z of horses

Author Don Harper
Editorial Manager Ruth Hooper
Editors Elise See Tai, Emily Hawkins
Art Director Miranda Kennedy
Art Editor Julia Harris
Production Director Clive Sparling
Consultant Zoologist Valerie Davies
Illustrators Michael Langham Rowe and Robin Carter,
The Art Agency (UK)

Created and produced by
Andromeda Children's Books
An imprint of Pinwheel Ltd
Winchester House
259–269 Old Marylebone Road
London
NW1 5XJ
UK
www.pinwheel.co.uk

This edition produced in 2006 for Scholastic Inc
Published by Tangerine Press, an imprint of Scholastic Inc;
557 Broadway; New York, NY 10012

Scholastic and Tangerine Press and associated logos are trademarks
of Scholastic Inc

ISBN 0-439-75458-5

Printed in USA

Information icons

Throughout this dictionary, there are special icons next
to each entry. These give you more information about
each horse.

Globes

These show you where each horse was first bred in
the world. Small red dots clearly show the location.

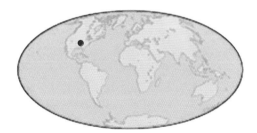

Size comparison pictures

Next to each entry you will see a symbol of an adult
human in front of a red icon of a horse. The symbol
shows you the size of each horse in real life.

The height of a horse is measured
in hands. One hand equals
4 inches (10 cm). The horse is
measured from the ground to
the top of the shoulders.

This symbol is an adult human.
The height of the human is
about 6 feet (1.8 m), so you
can compare the size of a horse
to the size of the human.

6 feet

HORSE
DICTIONARY

An A to Z of horses

tangerine Press®

an imprint of

■SCHOLASTIC

www.scholastic.com

Horses past and present

Today's horses are giants compared with their ancestors. The first recognizable horse, called Eohippus, was only the size of a small dog. It lived in the woodland of North America about 50 million years ago, where it fed on plants that grew near the ground. Eohippus had four separate toes on each of its front feet, and three toes on each hind foot, as well as pads like those on dogs' feet. Modern horses have just a single hoof on each foot.

Przewalski's horse

Horses take shape

Around 20 million years ago, America saw a period of dry weather that changed the appearance of the horse. The trees died out and the forests were replaced by huge areas of grassland. In this open country there was little cover to hide in. As new generations of horses were born, they had to grow bigger and more powerful in order to survive. Their legs were longer and this meant that they could see farther into the distance to spot danger. The central toe on each foot eventually developed into a hoof. This helped them to run faster to escape from predators. Horses' teeth also changed—they became larger so they could eat grass more easily.

Horses across the world

A million years ago, the direct ancestors of modern horses had developed. (They were probably very similar in appearance to Przewalski's horse—a small, wild horse that still survives.)

During this period, North America and Asia were joined by a stretch of land. Horses could easily cross into Asia and move from there into Europe and Africa. About 10,000 years ago, sea levels rose and cut off North America from Asia, and horses became extinct in the Americas. This may have been partly because of disease, and possibly also because of climate.

Horses today

In Europe and Asia horses thrived, and it was here that they were first domesticated by people. It was only about 600 years ago, once Europeans had settled in America, that horses were brought back to this part of the world. Some escaped into the wild, so now there are feral—or wild—herds living in North America, just as their ancestors would have done in the past. Modern horses are bred in several colors. Many are shades of brown that are given different names such as dun and bay.

Mustang

A horse's body

The shape of a horse's body will give you clues about why it was bred. A large, muscular horse is likely to have been used to pull carts. A horse that has been bred to ride will have a lighter body and a longer back. It will also have a long neck and sloping shoulders, with a deep chest.

Balance and shape

The appearance of a horse is described as its "conformation." A horse with good conformation has all its body parts in proportion. If a horse has bad conformation, its proportions are unbalanced. A weakness in one part of the horse's body is likely to be obvious elsewhere; if a horse's body is too narrow, this will cause its front legs to brush against each other when it runs.

Nails and shoes

Only part of a horse's foot is sensitive. The tough outer wall of the hoof is separated by a white line from the inner, sensitive area. A horse's shoes are fixed to the wall area using special nails. This does not cause pain.

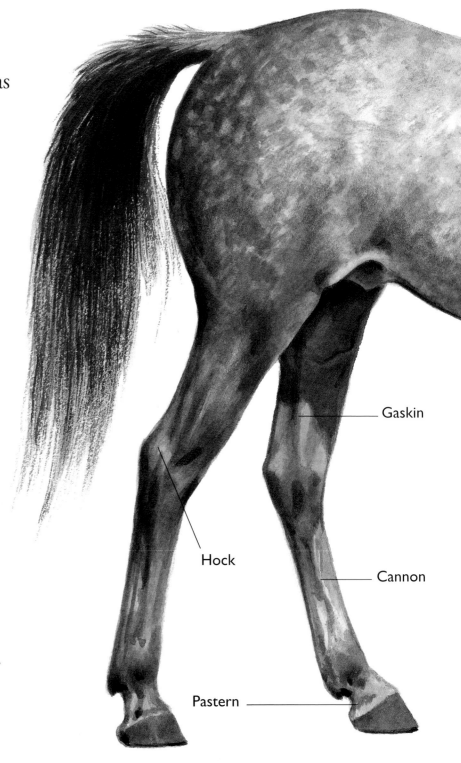

Gaskin

Hock

Cannon

Pastern

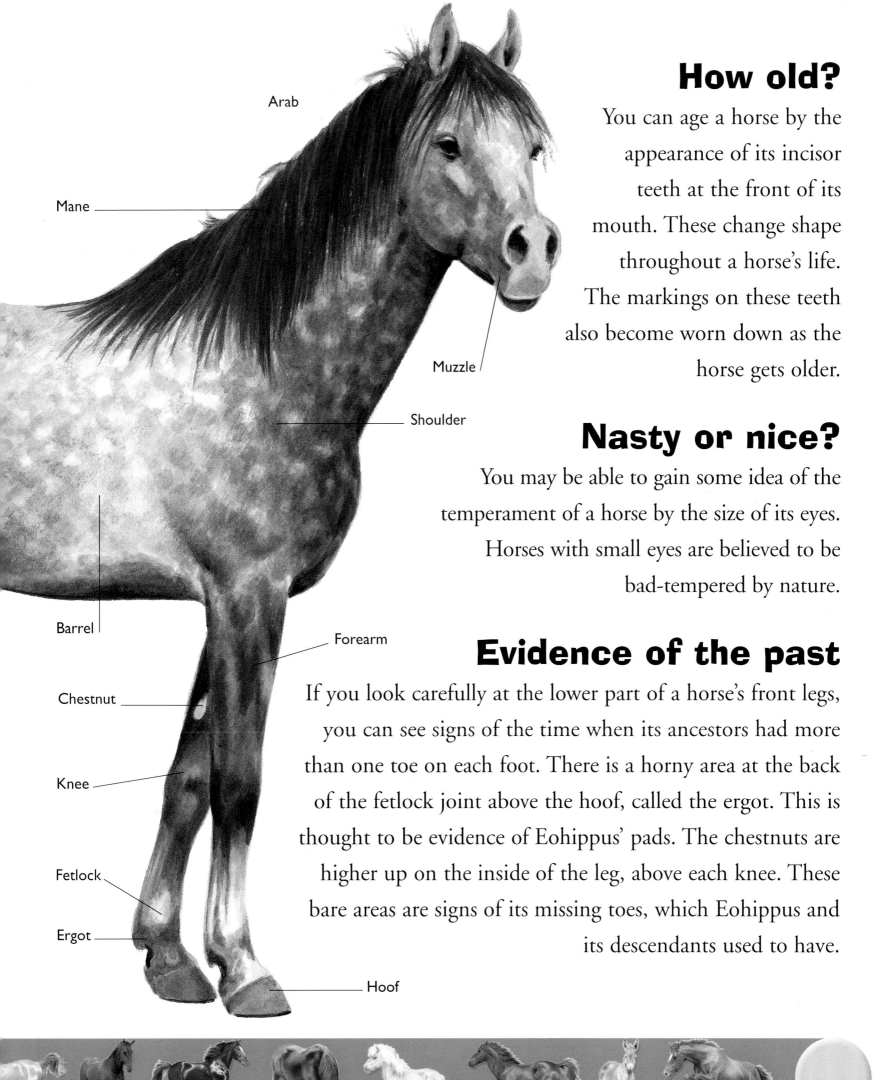

Arab

Mane

Muzzle

Shoulder

Barrel

Forearm

Chestnut

Knee

Fetlock

Ergot

Hoof

How old?

You can age a horse by the appearance of its incisor teeth at the front of its mouth. These change shape throughout a horse's life. The markings on these teeth also become worn down as the horse gets older.

Nasty or nice?

You may be able to gain some idea of the temperament of a horse by the size of its eyes. Horses with small eyes are believed to be bad-tempered by nature.

Evidence of the past

If you look carefully at the lower part of a horse's front legs, you can see signs of the time when its ancestors had more than one toe on each foot. There is a horny area at the back of the fetlock joint above the hoof, called the ergot. This is thought to be evidence of Eohippus' pads. The chestnuts are higher up on the inside of the leg, above each knee. These bare areas are signs of its missing toes, which Eohippus and its descendants used to have.

Aa

Max height: 15.2 hands (5 feet)

Appaloosa

The Appaloosa (pronounced a-pa-loo-sa) takes its name from the Palouse River that runs through northeastern Oregon, in the U.S. These spotted horses were first bred by an American Indian tribe called the Nez Perce, who lived in this area. This brave but gentle breed is now widely kept for riding purposes. The word "appaloosa" is used to describe a spotted coat patterning.

Arab

Max height: 15 hands (5 feet)

The Arab is the oldest domestic horse breed, prized for its speed as well as its stamina. Its skeleton is different from that of all other horses, as it has 17 rather than 18 ribs, and fewer bones make up its backbone. In the deserts of Asia, where grass can be hard to find, this horse sometimes eats insects called locusts, as well as dates.

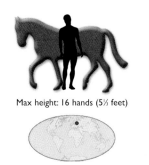

Max height: 16 hands (5½ feet)

Ardennes

This heavy horse comes from the Ardennes region on the border between France and Belgium. It was first used by the French army for riding and working. The Ardennes was crossbred with other heavy horses so it became bigger and stronger—it is now a powerful draft horse. It is often roan, where some white hairs are mixed with its base coat color.

Ass

Max height: 11 hands (3½ feet)

The ass is a wild relative of the donkey. The wild ass used to be common in Africa, but it is now endangered because of hunting. An ass differs from a horse because it makes a braying noise instead of neighing. Its mane is shorter than a horse's, and it does not have a chestnut—the small bare patch inside a horse's legs.

Max height: 14 hands (4½ feet)

Australian pony

British settlers took many different types of ponies when they moved to Australia 200 years ago. The Australian pony is a mix of various breeds, including the Shetland. It now looks most like the Welsh Mountain pony. It is often gray in color and is well-known for its friendly nature. It is a very popular children's riding pony.

Aa

Max height: 16 hands (5⅓ feet)

Australian Stock horse

Horses with great stamina were needed to work on the huge ranches of Australia, helping to herd cattle and sheep. Early horses used for this purpose became known as Walers, named after the southeastern Australian state of New South Wales. The faster and more athletic Australian Stock horse was bred by crossing Walers with Thoroughbreds.

Fact

The ancestors of the Australian Stock horse lived for up to a year on ships as they traveled from England to Australia.

Max height: 15.2 hands (5 feet)

Azteca

The Azteca is a new breed that was developed just over 30 years ago in Mexico. Its breeding has been carried out carefully using Quarter horses, Criollos, and another breed called Andalusians. The breeders have created a good-natured horse that can be ridden easily, can take part in competitions, and is also strong enough to do some farmwork.

Bb

Barb

Max height: 15 hands (5 feet)

The Barb is found in the desert area of northwest Africa and is one of the oldest breeds of horse. It is a strong horse, in spite of its small build and slim legs. The Barb is a fast sprinter and has good stamina, which allows it to run long distances.

Bashir Curly

Max height: 14 hands (4½ feet)

The Bashir Curly's coat can be so curly that it sometimes hangs down in ringlets. It sheds its entire mane and often much of its tail each summer. Wild horses of this type were first seen living near Austin, Texas in 1898. Nobody knows where they came from, but there is a similar breed in Asia—the Russian Bashir.

Bb

Max height: 16.2 hands (5½ feet)

Belgian Draft

This heavy horse is sometimes called the Brabant—the name of the area of Belgium where it was first kept. The Belgian Draft horse is very strong. It is able to pull carts loaded with heavy logs. The longer hair near the bottom of its legs is called "feathering."

Max height: 16 hands (5⅓ feet)

Boulonnais

The Boulonnais comes from northwest France, near Boulogne. This energetic, lively breed has a blotchy coat that is usually gray with darker patches. It is a strong, heavy horse with thick, powerful legs that help it carry out heavy farmwork, such as pulling carts.

Breton

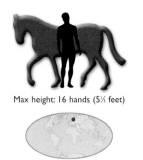

Max height: 16 hands (5½ feet)

The Breton is a very old breed of heavy horse that has been kept in northwest France for over 1,000 years. It is usually a shade of chestnut or chestnut-roan, with a flaxen mane and a short tail. As well as working on farms, the Breton has also been a warhorse. Today, it also takes part in driving competitions.

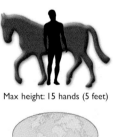

Fact
Breton horses were used to pull loads of seaweed that had gathered on Brittany's beaches. The seaweed was used as a fertilizer.

Brumby

Max height: 15 hands (5 feet)

The Brumby has lived wild in Australia for over 150 years. It is descended from domestic horses that escaped or were abandoned. These horses formed breeding herds, and their numbers quickly increased. The Brumby is shy and cannot be tamed easily, so it is not used for riding purposes. Most are quite small in size.

Cc

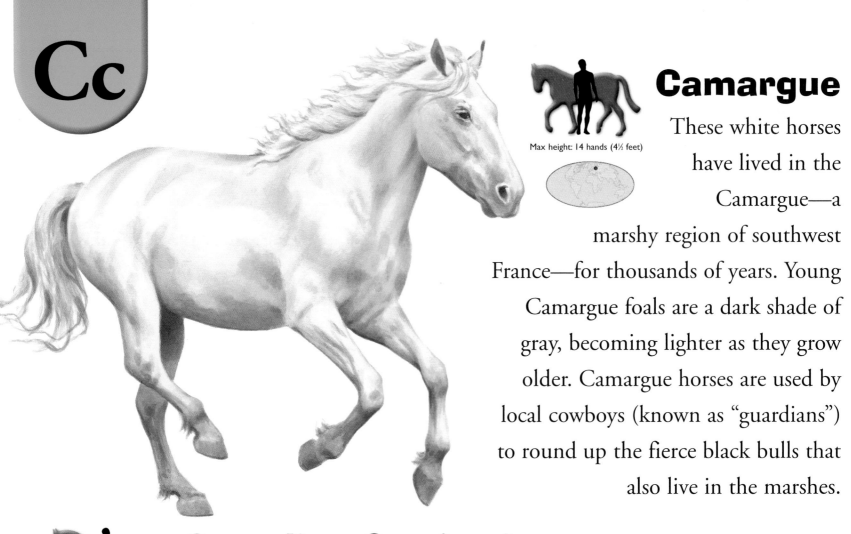

Max height: 14 hands (4½ feet)

Camargue

These white horses have lived in the Camargue—a marshy region of southwest France—for thousands of years. Young Camargue foals are a dark shade of gray, becoming lighter as they grow older. Camargue horses are used by local cowboys (known as "guardians") to round up the fierce black bulls that also live in the marshes.

Canadian Cutting horse

Max height: 16 hands (5⅓ feet)

The Canadian Cutting horse gets its name from its ability to drive or "cut" a particular cow out of a herd. It will stay with the cow, stopping it from rejoining the rest of the herd. This intelligent, agile horse looks similar to the American Quarter horse from which it is bred.

Cc

Caspian

Max height: 9 hands (3 feet)

People thought that these small horses were extinct until the breed was rediscovered in Iran (near the Caspian Sea) in 1965. Some believe that the Caspian is the original ancestor of the Arab, although the Arab's skeleton is different from that of all other breeds. The Caspian is a miniature horse rather than a pony, and is usually either bay or brown in color.

Fact
There were fewer than 50 Caspian horses still surviving when the breed was rediscovered.

Max height: 14 hands (4½ feet)

Cayuse Indian pony

This pony is different from other Native American breeds. It came from northwest Canada and was bred using French horses brought from Europe by the early settlers. The Cayuse Indians in this region started breeding these ponies. Sadly, the breed is now very scarce and is mainly limited to California.

Cc Chincoteague

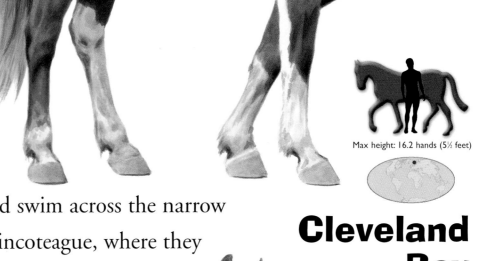

The islands of Assateague and Chincoteague lie off the coast of the U.S. state of Virginia.

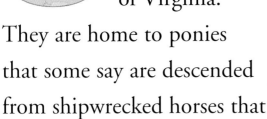

Max height: 12 hands (4 feet)

They are home to ponies that some say are descended from shipwrecked horses that swam ashore 400 years ago. Each year, the ponies are rounded up and swim across the narrow channel between the islands to Chincoteague, where they are sold. These intelligent, good-natured ponies are now found all over the U.S.

Max height: 16.2 hands (5½ feet)

Cleveland Bay

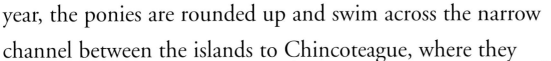

The Cleveland Bay horse was first bred in the area of Cleveland in northern England. The Cleveland Bay is closely linked to the British royal family. Today, it is used to pull royal carriages on important state occasions. Queen Elizabeth II has started a breeding program for these horses, because they are under threat of becoming extinct.

Max height: 18 hands (6 feet)

Clydesdale

This huge horse comes from the Clyde Valley in Scotland. It was taken to the U.S. more than 100 years ago, where it was used to pull heavy carts through city streets. Working teams of Clydesdales can still be seen at agricultural fairs. The Clydesdale may look like a Shire horse, but it has a longer neck and a much more lively stride.

Cob

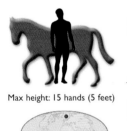

Max height: 15 hands (5 feet)

A Cob is not a breed of horse, but a type of horse—it was bred by crossing different breeds. The Cob's power and strength mean that it is a popular riding horse for men, because it can carry their weight easily. The mane of a Cob is often cut short, or "roached," to show its muscular neck more clearly.

Cc

Max height: 14.2 hands
(4¾ feet)

Connemara pony

The Connemara is named after an area on the west coast of Ireland, where it was first bred. It is the only breed of Irish pony. Connemaras were originally dun, but now they are more often gray, and sometimes even bay in color. The Connemara is very fast and is a good jumper. It is related to Celtic ponies, which lived wild in Europe thousands of years ago.

Max height: 15 hands (5 feet)

Criollo

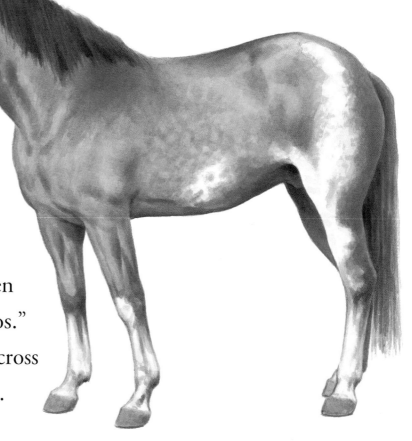

The Criollo is a tough breed that comes from Argentina. Its name means "Spanish horse," because it is descended from horses taken to Argentina from Spain more than 400 years ago. Criollos are ridden by South American cowboys called "gauchos." They help herd cattle over long distances across open grassland areas, known as the pampas.

Dales pony

Max height: 14.2 hands
(4¾ feet)

This pony comes from the Dales region of northern England. It is very strong, as it was bred to carry heavy containers of lead ore from mines on the moors. Today, the Dales pony is used to pull carts, and is also popular for general riding. It has a thick mane, long feathering on its lower legs, and is normally dark in color.

Danish Warmblood

Max height: 16.2 hands
(5½ feet)

This popular competition horse often takes part in jumping and dressage events. All Warmblood breeds are descended from Arab or Thoroughbred stock. The Danish Warmblood was bred by crossing Thoroughbreds with Frederiksborgs.

Dartmoor pony

Max height: 12 hands
(4 feet)

The moorland of southwest England is the original homeland of these friendly ponies. They are still found on Dartmoor today, but in smaller numbers than in the past. The Dartmoor has a quiet, reliable nature, and is a perfect choice for younger riders.

Dd
Ee

Donkey

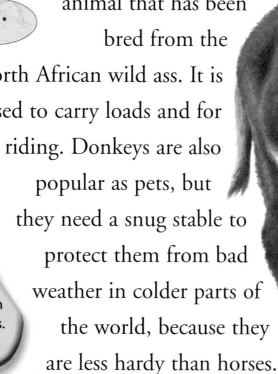

Max height: 11 hands (3½ feet)

The donkey is a domestic animal that has been bred from the North African wild ass. It is used to carry loads and for riding. Donkeys are also popular as pets, but they need a snug stable to protect them from bad weather in colder parts of the world, because they are less hardy than horses.

Fact

Donkeys have a much longer lifespan than horses. They can live for up to 50 years, but horses are unlikely to live for more than 30 years.

Max height: 12.3 hands (4 feet)

Exmoor pony

This pony's ancestors have lived on Exmoor in the southwest of England for 1,000 years. The pony is well protected against the rain and cold by its thick coat and a fan of short hairs at the top of its tail that stops ice from forming. This hardy, intelligent pony is often used for riding.

Falabella

Max height: 7 hands (2½ feet)

These tiny horses are named after the family who first bred them from small Spanish horses on a ranch in Argentina. The Falabella often seems to have quite a large head in contrast to the size of its body. It is sometimes used to pull tiny carts, and can even be ridden by small children.

Fell pony

Max height: 14 hands (4½ feet)

The Fell pony is a close relative of the Dales pony. They are similar in appearance, although the Fell does not have such a heavy body. Fell ponies are usually dark in color, but can be gray. The Fell is a very sure-footed pony, so it is perfect for riding. It is also used for driving.

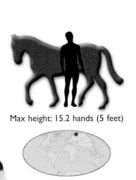

Max height: 15.2 hands (5 feet)

Finnish

The Finnish horse, also known as the Finnish universal, is used for many purposes. It is kept as a working horse on farms and often hauls heavy loads. Its pulling power comes from its muscular neck, powerful shoulders, and strong chest. This speedy horse is also popular for riding, show jumping, and harness racing.

Max height: 14 hands (4½ feet)

Fjord pony

This dun-colored pony is descended from Przewalski's horse. It has a dark stripe running down its back, which is a sign of its wild horse ancestry, along with the darker markings on its legs. Bred in Norway, the Fjord always has its mane cut short so its dark stripe stands above the paler hair of the rest of its mane.

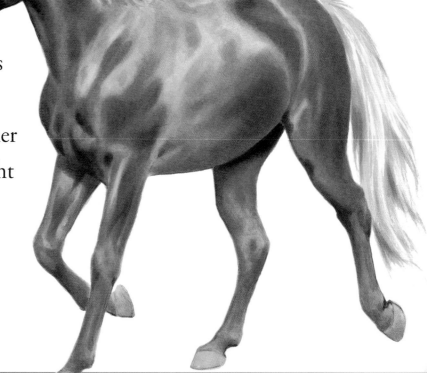

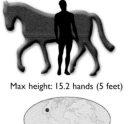

Max height: 15.2 hands (5 feet)

Florida Cracker

Florida Crackers are named after the sound of the whips used by cowboys who rode them to herd cattle. When cattle were moved into Florida from other states in the 1930s, they had to be caught regularly to be given medicine. This meant the cowboys needed a stronger, heavier horse than the Florida Cracker, so the breed became rare.

Max height: 16 hands (5½ feet)

Frederiksborg

This breed was created by King Frederick II of Denmark more than 500 years ago. The Frederiksborg (pronounced free-driks-borg) is always chestnut in color and often has white markings on its forehead and lower legs. It has been used for riding purposes and also to pull carriages. The Frederiksborg has a high action—it moves with its feet held high—and a short, upright neck.

Fact
Frederiksborg horses were all bred to be the same color so they looked like a team when pulling the royal carriages.

Friesian

Max height: 15 hands (5 feet)

The Friesian's ancestors were ridden hundreds of years ago by knights in battle. It is one of the oldest European breeds. The Friesian is named after the area of Friesland on the northern coast of the Netherlands, where this breed has been kept for centuries. It has a black coat and feathering around its feet, which is often seen in heavy horse breeds.

Gg

Max height: 14 hands (4½ feet)

Galiceno

This Mexican pony is descended from ponies that were bred in the Galicia region of northwest Spain. Its relatives were taken to the Americas by Spanish invaders more than 500 years ago. The Galiceno is a hardy, strong, and easily-trained pony with lots of stamina. It is often used on farms, where it helps herd cattle and pull carts.

Fact

All Galicenos are said to be directly descended from the very first group of horses that were seen in Mexico.

Max height: 16.2 hands (5½ feet)

Gelderlander

Named after the Dutch province of Gelder, the Gelderlander was bred there more than 100 years ago to pull carriages and work on farms, as well as for riding. Today, it often takes part in driving competitions. Many consider the Gelderlander to be an excellent show jumper.

Max height: 12.2 hands (4 feet)

Gotland pony

These ponies have lived on the Swedish island of Gotland for thousands of years. The breed is also known as the Skogsruss, meaning "little horse of the woods," because it is also found in the Lojsta forest on the mainland. It was used mainly for farmwork, but is now very popular for riding and jumping, as well as competing in trotting races.

Max height: 14 hands (4½ feet)

Hackney pony

The Hackney pony used to be called the Wilson pony, after its breeder, Christopher Wilson. It is a very hardy breed that comes from the moors of Cumbria in England's Lake District. This pony's "gait" (the way in which it moves) is unusual—it lifts its front legs very high with each step. It also holds its tail up high.

Hh

Max height: 14 hands (4½ feet)

Haflinger

The Haflinger is a breed of mountain pony that is named after the village of Hafling in the Austrian Tyrol, where it was first bred. It is nearly always chestnut in color, with a flaxen mane and tail. It pulls sleds in the winter and also works in the forests, hauling heavy logs.

Fact

Many Haflingers are branded with an image of an edelweiss flower, which is grown in its homeland.

Max height: 16.2 hands (5½ feet)

Hanoverian

The Hanoverian, named after an area of Germany, is a popular competition horse that is used for both show jumping and dressage. It is agile, athletic, and intelligent, so it can be trained quite easily. The Hanoverian is a result of crossbreeding between Holstein and Thoroughbred stock, more than 250 years ago.

Highland pony

Max height: 14.2 hands (4¾ feet)

Ponies have lived in Scotland for thousands of years. The Highland pony is the result of recent crossings between native ponies and French and Spanish horses. This long-haired breed is sure-footed with good stamina, so it is popular for trekking in the Highlands. It is also strong enough to haul logs out of the forests.

Holstein

Max height: 17 hands (5½ feet)

The Holstein was first kept as a coach horse, but when cars took over from horses, it was developed into a competition horse. This was achieved by crossbreeding with Thoroughbreds. The stamina and athletic ability of the Holstein mean that it is popular for cross-country racing. It also takes part in show jumping competitions.

Hh Ii

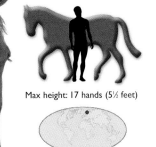

Max height: 17 hands (5½ feet)

Hunter

The Hunter is not a true breed, but a type of horse bred to suit its local countryside. Hunters that are ridden over flat, open country need to be fast, whereas on rougher ground, more strength is needed. Most Hunters are based on crosses between Thoroughbreds and Irish Draft horses, often with some mixing with the Cleveland Bay or similar breeds.

Fact
Although Hunters jump very well, some are also ridden on the flat in side-saddle classes at some shows.

Max height: 13.2 hands (4½ feet)

Icelandic pony

The relatives of this breed were taken to Iceland more than 1,000 years ago. No other horse breed has such a pure bloodline as the Icelandic pony. Instead of the usual four gaits, this horse has six—including the "pace," where both feet on one side leave the ground at the same time, and a fast running walk called the "tolt."

Irish Draft

Max height: 17 hands (5½ feet)

The Irish Draft horse was used to carry out many different tasks on farms. Its strength and size come from heavy horses brought to Ireland from France about 1,000 years ago. Today's Irish Draft horses are taller than in the past, and are kept mainly for riding rather than working. They have strong legs and jump well over fences.

Italian Heavy Draft

Max height: 16 hands (5½ feet)

From northern Italy, the Italian Heavy Draft horse has a strong, muscular body. It is still used for farmwork and as a draft horse (for pulling carts). Italian Heavy Draft horses are often chestnut in color, and some are roan.

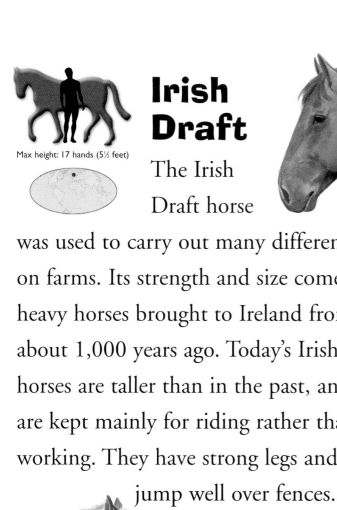

Jj
Kk

Max height: 15.3 hands (5 feet)

Jutland

The Jutland is named after the area of Denmark where it was first bred. These powerful, heavy horses are closely related to the Suffolk Punch. Teams of Jutlands can still be seen at shows pulling carts, just as they did before trucks existed. Like other heavy horses, the Jutland is a gentle giant with a friendly nature.

Fact
The Jutland is descended from a Shire X Suffolk stallion (see X-bred, p. 57) who was bred in Britain and taken to Denmark in 1862.

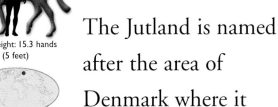

Max height: 15.2 hands (5 feet)

Kabardin

Bay or black in color, the Kabardin comes from the Caucasus mountains of Russia. Its feet are very hard, so it can be ridden without shoes. The Kabardin is sure-footed, even when walking on sloping, stony ground, and it has great stamina. It also has a keen sense of direction, so it can find its way home after dark or in heavy snow.

Karabakh

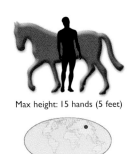

Max height: 15 hands (5 feet)

Found in Azerbaijan in Asia, the Karabakh (pronounced kar-a-bak) is named after the mountains there. This horse can be an unusual metallic shade of chestnut, sometimes with white markings. It is used in a number of sports that are popular in the region, including a type of mounted basketball called "surpamakh," as well as "chavgan," which is like polo.

Max height: 14.3 hands (4¾ feet)

Kathiawari

The Kathiawari (pronounced ka-tee-a-wa-ree) is unusual because its large ears curve inward until they almost touch each other. This ancient breed comes from the Kathiawar peninsula, which juts out on the west side of India. The Kathiawari's ancestors were Arab horses brought to India by ship, which bred with various native horses.

Kk

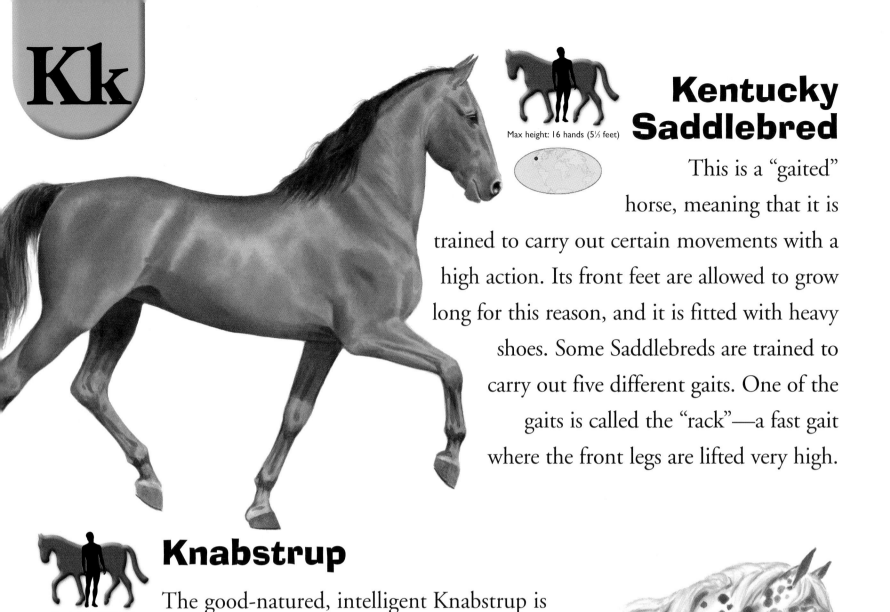

Kentucky Saddlebred

Max height: 16 hands (5⅓ feet)

This is a "gaited" horse, meaning that it is trained to carry out certain movements with a high action. Its front feet are allowed to grow long for this reason, and it is fitted with heavy shoes. Some Saddlebreds are trained to carry out five different gaits. One of the gaits is called the "rack"—a fast gait where the front legs are lifted very high.

Knabstrup

Max height: 15.2 hands (5 feet)

The good-natured, intelligent Knabstrup is named after the estate in Denmark where the breed was developed. All Knabstrups have a spotted patterning that extends down their legs. Their markings mean that individual horses can be recognized very easily. The Knabstrup has been trained both as a circus horse and for stunt riding.

Landais

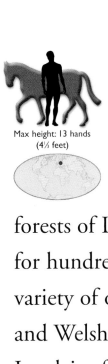

Max height: 13 hands (4⅓ feet)

The Landais' ancestors roamed free in the forests of Landes, in southwest France, for hundreds of years. They bred with a variety of other horses, including Arabs and Welsh ponies. As a result, today's Landais often differ in height depending on their bloodline. The breed has become very popular in France as a children's riding pony.

Max height: 16 hands (5⅓ feet)

Latvian

Latvian horses come from Latvia, a country on the Baltic Sea. There are three different types of Latvian horses. The lightweight Latvian is used mainly for riding, whereas the standard is a heavy horse, used for pulling carts. The third type is thought to be the oldest. It is called the Latvian light harness horse.

Ll

Max height: 16.2 hands (5½ feet)

Lipizzaner

The famous "white" stallions that perform in displays by the Spanish Riding School (based in Austria) are Lipizzaners. They are actually pale gray in color. Some are born bay in color, and traditionally one bay is always included in a troupe of Lipizzaners. Other colors, such as dun, existed up until 300 years ago.

Max height: 16 hands (5⅓ feet)

Lusitano

This Portuguese breed is named after the country where it was first bred—Portugal used to be called Lusitania. The Lusitano was first used as a warhorse and, because it is very agile, it is a good horse for riding purposes. It is often gray in color, but can also be chestnut or bay, and has a distinctive curved, or "Roman," nose.

Fact
The Lusitano is ridden in Portuguese bullfighting contests, so it needs to move very quickly to escape from the angry bull.

Maremmana

Max height: 15.3 hands (5 feet)

This breed comes from Maremma in the Italian district of Tuscany. Groups of these horses can still be seen in a semi-wild state in this area. The Maremmana is often kept for farmwork, especially for herding cattle. It is fast and agile, so it is sometimes used for show jumping.

Missouri Fox Trotter

Max height: 16.2 hands (5½ feet)

Bred in the Ozark mountains in the 1820s, the Missouri Fox Trotter is one of the oldest native breeds of horse in the U.S. It is called a Fox Trotter because of its unusual gait—it appears to walk with its front legs and trot with its hind legs, which makes it comfortable to ride for long periods. For this reason, it became popular with ranchers, although it was first bred as a racehorse.

Mm

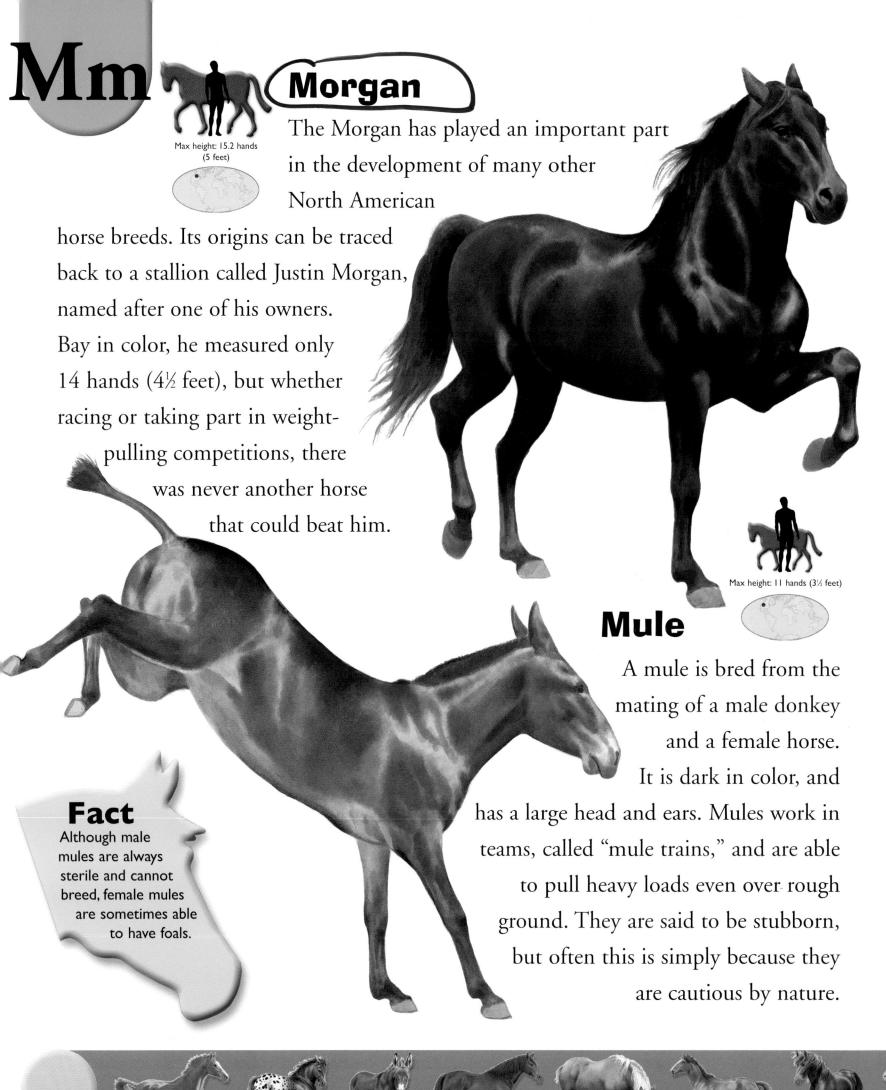

Max height: 15.2 hands
(5 feet)

Morgan

The Morgan has played an important part in the development of many other North American horse breeds. Its origins can be traced back to a stallion called Justin Morgan, named after one of his owners. Bay in color, he measured only 14 hands (4½ feet), but whether racing or taking part in weight-pulling competitions, there was never another horse that could beat him.

Max height: 11 hands (3½ feet)

Mule

A mule is bred from the mating of a male donkey and a female horse. It is dark in color, and has a large head and ears. Mules work in teams, called "mule trains," and are able to pull heavy loads even over rough ground. They are said to be stubborn, but often this is simply because they are cautious by nature.

Fact

Although male mules are always sterile and cannot breed, female mules are sometimes able to have foals.

Murgese

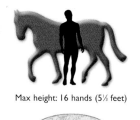

Max height: 16 hands (5⅓ feet)

Murgese horses come from the Murge region in southeast Italy, and many of them still roam the forests, finding their own food. The Murgese has a broad, sloping nose and is usually black in color. In the past, it was ridden by soldiers as a cavalry horse. Today, some Murgese horses still work on farms, while others are kept for riding.

Mustang

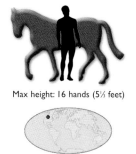

Max height: 16 hands (5⅓ feet)

The mustang is a "feral" (wild) horse that lives in North America. Its ancestors were domestic horses that escaped or were turned loose and started breeding in the wild. Its name comes from the Spanish word "mesteth," meaning "band of horses." Mustangs are shy and not easy to approach. They live in herds made up of one stallion and several mares.

Nn

New Forest pony

Max height: 14.2 hands (4¾ feet)

These ponies still roam freely through the New Forest, in the English county of Hampshire, just as their ancestors did more than 1,000 years ago. There is limited grazing, so the number of ponies is kept to about 2,500. Each year, the herds are rounded up and some ponies are sold at special auctions.

Fact
New Forest ponies are not fenced in, but can roam across the heathland where they live, sometimes even walking along roads.

Nonius

Max height: 16.2 hands (5½ feet)

The founder of this breed was a stallion called Nonius Senior, who was captured in a battle in France in the 1800s when he was three years old. He was taken to a stud in Hungary, where he fathered many foals. Crosses with Thoroughbreds have improved the conformation (physical appearance) of the breed.

Noriker

Max height: 17 hands (5½ feet)

The Noriker is a very old breed of heavy horse. It is named after the ancient Roman state of Noricum—now known as Austria. In the past, the Noriker's relatives were used as warhorses, because their size and strength frightened enemies. Today, the breed is still very strong, with powerful legs and a very deep girth. Most Norikers are chestnut or bay.

North Swedish horse

Max height: 15.3 hands (5 feet)

The small size and great strength of the North Swedish horse mean that it is well suited to pulling logs in the forests of Sweden, or working on farms. Both mares and stallions are always checked very carefully for illness or injury to make sure that their foals will be strong and healthy.

Oo

Max height: 17.2 hands (5¾ feet)

Oldenburg

The Oldenburg is named after the province of Germany where it was first bred more than 400 years ago. It was used as a carriage horse, often by the mail service. Crosses with Thoroughbreds changed the appearance and action of the Oldenburg. It became lighter and developed a lower action. Today, Oldenbergs often take part in dressage and driving competitions.

Fact
Each October, young Oldenburg stallions take part in tests that last for three days, to decide which ones will be used for breeding.

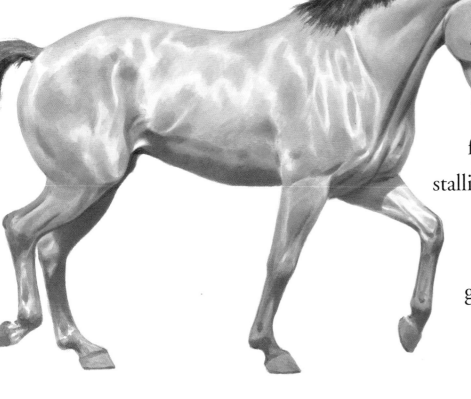

Max height: 16 hands (5⅓ feet)

Orlov Trotter

A Russian Count called Alexi Orlov first bred these horses. He won a famous battle and was given a gray Arab stallion called Smetanka—the ancestor of all Orlov Trotters. Today, more than 200 years later, most Orlov Trotters are still gray, although some are brown. They are lightly built, tall, and often take part in trotting races, pulling a cart and rider.

Paint horse

Max height: 16 hands (5⅓ feet)

The Paint horse was bred from Spanish horses with white markings that were taken to the Americas by European explorers. Some Paint horses have jagged white markings on the sides of their bodies. This coloring is called "overo patterning." Others have "tobiano patterning," where the coat is white with large spots of color.

Palomino

Max height: 16 hands (5⅓ feet)

The name Palomino comes from a Spanish golden grape. Many horse breeds have palomino coloration, but now breeders are trying to create a distinctive breed with this coloring, using Quarter horses, Arabs, and Thoroughbreds. Some Palominos are darker than others, but all have a silvery mane and tail.

Pp

Max height: 17.2 hands (5¼ feet)

Percheron

These massive horses come from the La Perche area in Normandy, France. They were bred by crossing Norman Cobs with Arabs. Unlike most heavy horses, the Percheron has very little feathering on its lower legs. Percherons were once used by French knights in battle. They have also been used as carthorses, worked on farms, and can even be ridden.

Fact
The Percheron nearly died out in the U.S. when tractors took over, but it survived thanks to the Amish who continued to use it for farming.

Max height: 15.2 hands (5 feet)

Peruvian Paso

The Peruvian Paso is also called the Peruvian Stepping horse because of its unusual gait. It is very comfortable to ride, even over uneven ground. This horse was bred mainly from Barbs crossed with Andalucians (a Spanish breed). Its ancestors were taken to Peru more than 500 years ago.

Max height: 15.1 hands (5 feet)

Polo pony

These horses have been specially bred to take part in the game of polo. They need to be strong enough to carry an adult rider, and agile enough to turn in tight circles. In the breeding of Polo ponies, Thoroughbreds have been used for their speed and Criollos have helped to give strength.

Fact
A Polo pony must have a smooth action to allow its rider to hit the ball without difficulty.

Max height: 14 hands (4½ feet)

Pony of the Americas

The spotted coat of the Pony of the Americas can be traced back to the Appaloosa mare that founded this breed just over 50 years ago when she was crossed with a Shetland stallion. Other relatives of the Pony of the Americas include Quarter horses and Arabs. It is a very popular choice as a riding pony for children.

Pp Pottock

This pony comes from the Basque region on the border between Spain and France. The name Pottock means "small horse." It has been used to carry goods through this mountainous area for many years and it can also be ridden. The Pottock has a dip in its skull between the eyes, suggesting that it may be descended from Arab stock.

Max height: 14.2 hands (4¾ feet)

Przewalski's horse

Max height: 12 hands (4 feet)

Named after a famous Russian explorer, this pony-like animal is the only true wild horse left in the world. It lives in Asia, but nearly died out in the early 1900s because it was hunted. Luckily, Przewalski's horses have been bred in zoos, and some of their offspring have been released back into the wild in a special reserve in Mongolia.

Max height: 12 hands (4 feet)

Quagga

The Quagga was a type of zebra that used to live in South Africa. It became extinct because it was heavily hunted. Unlike other zebras, its stripes were only on the front half of its body. Experiments have crossed a mule with a zebra and have produced an animal with a gray coat, without the head and neck stripes.

Max height: 16 hands (5⅓ feet)

Quarter horse

The Quarter horse has become the most common breed of horse in the world today. It was first bred as a racehorse, and used to sprint over a course that was a quarter of a mile long. Since then, the Quarter horse has been used for many different purposes, including riding, cattle work, polo, and racing.

Rr

Rangerbred

Max height: 16 hands (5⅓ feet)

The Rangerbred is also called the Colorado Ranger. It is descended from two stallions, an Arab and a Barb, which were given as a gift to General Ulysses S. Grant, a famous commander in the American Civil War. The Rangerbred has a spotted pattern and is kept as a riding horse. It is also used on ranches to herd cattle.

Rhinelander

Max height: 16.2 hands (5½ feet)

The Rhinelander was bred from the Rhineland Heavy Draft horse, a horse that became less popular when farmers started using machines. Crossings between this heavy horse, Thoroughbreds, and Hanoverians have developed the Rhinelander, which is a riding horse rather than a draft horse.

Fact
The Rhinelander is one of several German breeds that have been developed into popular competition horses.

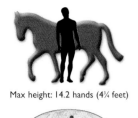

Max height: 14.2 hands (4¾ feet)

Riding pony

The riding pony is not a pure breed, but a type of pony. It was created in Britain from a number of different breeds, including Welsh ponies. Some small horses, especially Thoroughbreds and Arabs, have also been used in its development. As a result of this, the riding pony's height is quite variable.

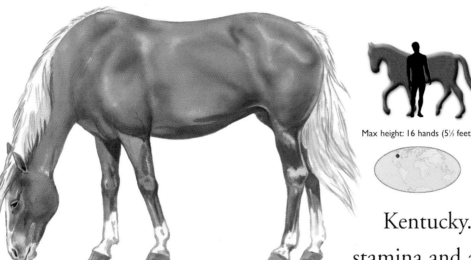

Max height: 16 hands (5⅓ feet)

Rocky Mountain horse

The Rocky Mountain horse was first bred in the U.S. state of Kentucky. This excellent riding horse has great stamina and a very smooth gait, even over uneven ground. It is often a chocolate-brown color with a flaxen mane and tail.

Max height: 16 hands (5⅓ feet)

Rottaler

The Rottaler is a very old breed, also called the Bavarian Warmblood. Chestnut in color, it was first used as a warhorse hundreds of years ago. The Rottaler still has a powerful body, but it is lighter today than in the past because of crossings with Thoroughbreds. This means that the Rottaler is faster than it used to be, so it is a good competition horse.

Ss

Sable Island pony

Max height: 14 hands (4½ feet)

These ponies live on Sable Island, off the coast of Nova Scotia on the eastern side of Canada. They are thought to be relatives of Norman horses that were brought to the island nearly 300 years ago. Today, most Sable Island ponies live in semi-wild herds, but young foals can be tamed and make good riding ponies when they are older.

Saddlebred

Max height: 16 hands (5½ feet)

The Saddlebred is very popular among the American "gaited" breeds. It has a very high action, and can be taught to perform extra paces for dressage competitions. The Saddlebred is also popular for trail riding because it gives a smooth ride even over rough ground.

Shagya

Max height: 15 hands (5 feet)

This breed is named after a famous Arab stallion called Shagya, who was brought to a stud in Hungary from the Middle Eastern country of Syria. Today, the Shagya still looks very similar to an Arab, but it is larger. It was used as a cavalry horse, but is now seen in riding competitions.

Fact
The careful breeding program of some Shagyas can be traced back over more than 20 generations.

Shetland pony

Max height: 10 hands (3½ feet)

Short but strong, the Shetland is a very popular children's riding pony. It is named after the islands off the northeast coast of Scotland, where its ancestors have lived for up to 10,000 years. The Shetland was useful to the islanders because it helped them to carry heavy sacks of peat that had been dug out of the ground for fuel.

Ss

Shire

Max height: 18 hands (6 feet)

First bred in England, the Shire horse is the biggest of the heavy horses. It is incredibly strong with a very friendly nature. This breed's history dates back to the medieval Great Horse that used to carry knights in heavy armor. Today, the Shire is kept as a draft horse (for pulling carts), and also takes part in ploughing competitions at agricultural shows.

Suffolk Punch

Max height: 16 hands (5⅓ feet)

Unlike many heavy horses, the Suffolk Punch has very little feathering around its feet. This helps keep its legs free from mud while it is working. This breed comes from the county of Suffolk in southeast England. It is used for farmwork, including ploughing. All Suffolk Punches are chestnut in color.

Sumba

Max height: 12.2 hands (4 feet)

The Sumba pony is named after its native Indonesian island, which lies to the south of mainland Asia. These ponies are often trained for dance competitions where they are ridden bareback with bells on their knees. The rider makes sure that the pony moves to the rhythm of a beating drum. Sumba ponies are also used in some sporting competitions.

Fact

Swedish Warmbloods often compete at the Olympic Games. One stallion, called Drabant, had six sons taking part in 1960.

Swedish Warmblood

Max height: 16.2 hands (5½ feet)

Many different breeds of horse were used to create the Swedish Warmblood. It was first used in battles as a cavalry horse, and is now very popular as a competition horse. Its calm nature means that it does well in dressage competitions. The height and strength of the Swedish Warmblood also mean that it can jump very well.

Tt

Max height: 13 hands (4⅓ feet)

Tarpan

The Tarpan was a wild ancestor of many of today's breeds of light horse. It was dun in color, but its coat turned white in the winter, helping it to hide in the snowy countryside. The last true Tarpans died out in Poland in 1879, but soon after this, a herd was recreated from Tarpan crossbreeds that still existed.

Max height: 16 hands (5⅓ feet)

Tennessee Walking horse

Coming from the southern state of Tennessee, this walking horse has a very unusual walking gait inherited from a stallion called Black Allan. As well as its two walking paces, the Tennessee Walking horse also canters very smoothly. This horse is a comfortable ride, as well as being fast. It is sometimes black in color, just like Black Allan.

Tersk

Max height: 15 hands (5 feet)

The Tersk comes from
the Caucasus Mountains
of Asia and is descended from Arab
stock. It is named after the stud
where it was first bred. The Tersk is
fast enough to outrun Arabs and has
enough strength and jumping ability
to win endurance competitions.

Thoroughbred

Max height: 16.2 hands
(5½ feet)

Bred for speed, the Thoroughbred is often known
simply as the racehorse. Today's Thoroughbreds can
be traced back to three different stallions, called the
Byerley Turk, the Darley Arab, and the Godolphin Arab. They were crossed with
running horses that were popular in England about 300 years ago, which helped
to improve their conformation and pace.

Trakehner

Max height: 17.2 hands (5¾ feet)

The Trakehner (pronounced tra-kay-ner)
is an old Polish breed that used to carry
knights into battle. Later, it was used to
pull carriages, and was also trained by the army as
a cavalry horse. Crosses with Thoroughbreds gave it a more
athletic appearance, and it is now a good competition horse.
Today's Trakehner has speed, stamina, and good jumping ability.

Uu
Vv

Max height: 16.1 hands (5⅓ feet)

Ukrainian Saddle horse

A lot of care is taken over the breeding of the Ukrainian Saddle horse. These horses are kept for riding, and tested for their speed, stamina, and jumping ability. Only the top performers are used for breeding. The Ukrainian Saddle horse is partly descended from the extinct Russian Saddle horse.

Max height: 14.2 hands (4¾ feet)

Viatka

The Viatka is a rare breed of pony named after an area of Russia. It has a very thick winter coat to protect it against the cold. The Viatka is often either bay or chestnut roan in color. It is used for many tasks, such as riding, pulling carts, and helping on farms.

Max height: 16 hands (5½ feet)

Vladimir Heavy Draft

This horse is related to the Clydesdale and other similar British breeds, such as Suffolk Punch, Shire, and Cleveland Bay. The Vladimir (pronounced vla-dee-meer) Heavy Draft horse is named after the area in Russia where it was bred more than 100 years ago. It is often used to pull special carts known in Russia as "troikas."

Max height: 15.2 hands (5 feet)

Welsh Cob

The Welsh Cob is a large, strong Welsh pony. It was often used to pull carts in Wales. The strength of the Welsh Cob meant that it could also pull gun carriages in wartime, and could be ridden by soldiers. Today, the Welsh Cob is likely to be seen in driving and dressage competitions.

Ww

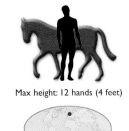

Max height: 12 hands (4 feet)

Welsh Mountain pony

The ancestors of the sure-footed Welsh Mountain pony have lived in the hills of Wales for more than 2,000 years. The Welsh Mountain pony has a tough, hardy nature. It is the smallest and oldest of the Welsh breeds and was used to create both the Welsh pony and the Welsh Cob. It always has a solid color.

Westphalian

Max height: 17 hands (5½ feet)

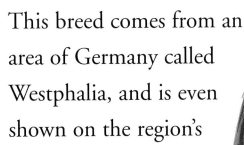

This breed comes from an area of Germany called Westphalia, and is even shown on the region's coat-of-arms. It is descended from heavy farm horses that were crossed with lighter horses, including another German Warmblood called the Hanoverian. The Westphalian is a large, good-natured breed that is often seen in dressage and show jumping competitions.

Max height: 16.2 hands (5½ feet)

Wielkopolski

The Wielkopolski (pronounced v-yel-ko-pol-skee) is descended from two old Polish breeds called the Pozan and Masuren, which are now extinct. Other breeds, especially Thoroughbreds and Arabs, helped make this breed more athletic. The Wielkopolski is a good event horse and is popular for show jumping and general riding. Some are still used on farms, too.

X-bred

When two horses of different breeds have a foal, this is known as a crossbreed. The "X" represents the cross, such as the Arab X Thoroughbred, where the stallion is written first. The foal is likely to show characteristics of both its parents, but there is no way of predicting what its height will be, especially if its parents vary in size themselves.

Yy Zz

Max height: 14.3 hands (4¾ feet)

Yakut pony

The Yakut comes from a region called Yakutia in Siberia. It is possible that the Yakut is descended from an old breed called the Tundra horse. It can survive well in its harsh climate because its hair becomes much thicker and longer in winter to protect it against the cold. The local people rely on these horses not just for transport, but also for milk.

Max height: 13 hands (4½ feet)

Zebra

These wild members of the horse family live on the plains of Africa. There are three species, which can be told apart by differences in their striped markings. Within a herd, zebras recognize each other by their stripes. When seen from a distance, these stripes help a zebra blend in with its surroundings, so it is less obvious to predators.

Max height: 12 hands (4 feet)

Zedonk

A Zedonk is the result of a mating between a zebra stallion and a female donkey. Their foals can also be called zonkeys and zeasses. Most Zedonks have striped legs like a zebra, but the body color of a donkey, with a dark stripe running down the center of the back. A Zedonk is quicker but harder to train than a donkey.

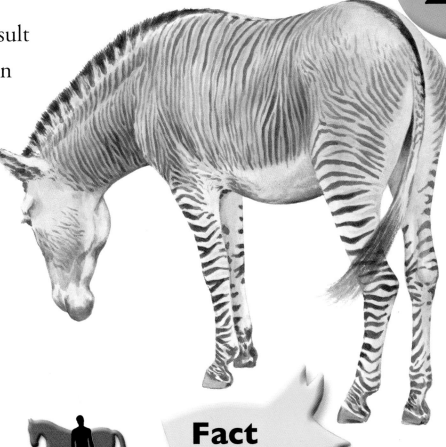

Max height: 14.2 hands (4¾ feet)

Fact
The Zemaituka sometimes has a stripe running down its back from its mane. This and its dun coloring show that it is closely related to wild horses.

Zemaituka

There are very few of these small horses left in their native country of Lithuania. The origins of the Zemaituka, also called the Zihund, go back to the wild Tarpan. The Zemaituka is very hardy, because it must be able to survive in an area where the winters are bitterly cold. It is used on farms and for general riding purposes.

Glossary

Action A description of the way in which a horse moves; a horse with a high action lifts its legs farther than one with a low action.

Ancestors/ancestry Two or more breeds that were mated together to create a new breed; older relatives of an animal, which may be extinct.

Appaloosa The spotted patterning associated with native North American Indian horse breeds.

Bay A horse that has a reddish-brown color, with black legs, mane, and tail. Also describes a type of horse with this color.

Bloodline The horses from which a particular individual is descended, extending back over a number of generations.

Bray The harsh noise that an ass or donkey makes.

Breed A group of horses with recognizable characteristics in common, in terms of their appearance and size.

Breeding The mating of horses or other equids (horses, asses, zebras, and related extinct animals), with the aim of producing offspring.

Cavalry Horses that are ridden by soldiers into battle.

Chestnut This describes the variable golden color seen in horses, ranging from pale gold to reddish-gold. It also describes the dry, hairless area above the inside of the knees on the front and hind legs, which are the remains of the horse's missing digits.

Coldblood A heavy horse whose ancestry includes the ancient forest horse of Europe.

Conformation The way in which the different parts of the horse's body come together to create its overall appearance. A horse with poor conformation is not a good example of its breed, and is unlikely to work well.

Glossary

Crossbreed Offspring resulting from the mating of two breeds, or between a domestic and wild member of the horse family.

Domesticated A member of the horse family that is kept and bred by people.

Draft A member of the horse family used to pull a cart of any type, as well as heavy weights, such as logs.

Dray A type of cart often used to deliver beer. The heavy horses that pulled it are often known as dray horses.

Dressage A style of riding where the horse follows its rider's movements. Dressage competitions are often carried out to music.

Driving The act of pulling a cart, under instructions from the driver. Today, this is often a competitive sport.

Dun A variable color in horses, which can either be yellowish, grayish-brown, or even bluish.

Endangered Describes a breed or species that has such a small population that it is in danger of becoming extinct.

Endurance The ability of horses to compete against each other over long distances, where stamina is important.

Extinct A species or breed of horse that no longer exists, having died out.

Feathering The longer hair present on the lower part of the legs, often seen in breeds of heavy horse.

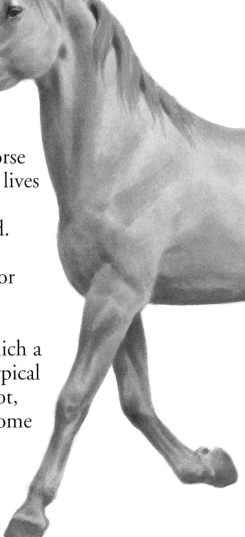

Feral A domestic horse that has escaped and lives wild, breeding with others to form a herd.

Flaxen A yellowish or cream color.

Gait The way in which a horse moves. Four typical gaits are the walk, trot, canter, and gallop. Some horses may display other gaits.

Glossary

Gaucho The name given to South American cowboys who work on ranches and herd cattle on horseback.

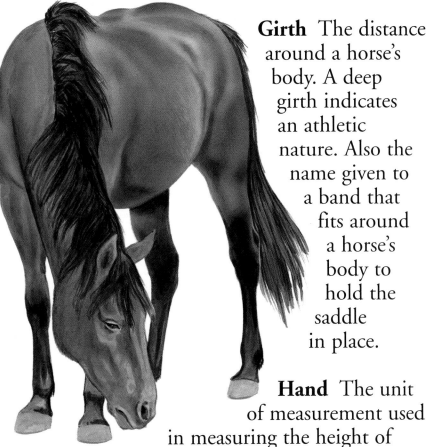

Girth The distance around a horse's body. A deep girth indicates an athletic nature. Also the name given to a band that fits around a horse's body to hold the saddle in place.

Hand The unit of measurement used in measuring the height of horses and ponies. One hand is equivalent to 4 inches (10 cm).

Hardy Able to survive well outdoors during periods of bad weather.

Heavy horse A horse defined by its large, muscular body; used for work rather than riding.

Light horse A horse with a lighter conformation; used for riding rather than pulling loads.

Mane The long area of hair extending from the back of the head down the neck.

Mare A female horse or pony.

Native A member of a horse family that occurs naturally in that particular area.

Pace A type of stepping in horses where the legs on the same side are lifted together. Pace can also be a description of the speed at which a horse moves.

Palomino A horse with a golden coat and a white mane and tail. This color can occur in various breeds, but is best known in the case of the Palomino breed itself.

Pony A small member of the horse family measuring less than 14.2 hands (4¾ feet).

Glossary

Sure-footed The ability of a horse or pony to move over uneven ground without stumbling.

Team A group of horses working together, often pulling a heavy weight.

Type Horses that have been created for a particular purpose, but which do not form a recognizable breed, or necessarily share a common ancestry.

Warhorse A heavy horse used to carry a knight in armor into battle.

Warmblood Describes a horse that has some Arab or Thoroughbred blood in its ancestry.

Ranch An extensive farmstead, where livestock are allowed to roam over the land, being herded by riders on horseback.

Roached The way in which the mane is cut off, as often seen in Cobs and Polo ponies.

Roan A red, chestnut, or black coat interspersed with white hairs, creating red, strawberry, and blue roan patterning.

Stallion A male horse or pony.

Stamina The ability not to become tired too quickly.

Stud A place where stallions are kept to mate with mares. Also, can be used to describe a particular stallion.

Index